PETER SHAFFER

PETER SHAFFER

by

JOHN RUSSELL TAYLOR

Edited by Ian Scott-Kilvert

PUBLISHED FOR
THE BRITISH COUNCIL
BY LONGMAN GROUP LTD

LONGMAN GROUP LTD
Longman House, Burnt Mill, Harlow, Essex

*Associated companies, branches and
representatives throughout the world*

First published 1974
© John Russell Taylor 1974

*Printed in Scotland by
Her Majesty's Stationery Office at HMSO Press, Edinburgh*

ISBN O 582 01231 7

PETER SHAFFER

DURING the years of the so-called New Drama in Britain we became used, almost to the point of being blasé, to dramatists making sensational débuts. From John Osborne on, the norm was a public career starting with a bang, a flash, outrage or incomprehension, conspicuous originality of some kind, either of subject-matter or of technique, and then a gradual easing into orthodoxy, achieved as a rule more by a change in the public's expectations and received ideas about what drama should and should not be than through some compromise in the direction of conformity on the part of the writer himself. But this pattern in contemporary arts, though frequent, is not necessarily standard. Some are born original, some achieve originality, and some have originality thrust upon them. If we think of music, for example, we can find many cases, like those of Schoenberg and Scriabin, where the beginnings are thoroughly conventional and only by a slow process of trial and error, of deliberate stylistic experimentation, does the creative originality of the artist evolve and make itself evident.

So it is with Peter Shaffer. He began his public career with a major success: *Five Finger Exercise*, one of the biggest critical and commercial successes of the New Drama in its early days. But so conservative did it seem in its dramaturgy, so familiar in its subject matter and background to an audience nurtured on Terence Rattigan, that there was serious, if rather pointless, argument about whether the play and its author could be considered really to belong to the New Drama at all, except by a chronological accident. At the time of the play's production, Peter Shaffer was thirty-two; he was born in 1926, which placed him about midway in the generation of playwrights coming forward at that time—three or four years older than John Osborne, Harold Pinter and John Arden, two or three years younger than Robert Bolt, Brendan Behan and John Mortimer.

As a person, Shaffer was and has remained one of the most mysterious of his generation. Many of his contemporaries had contrived, or just happened, to become public figures, their opinions canvassed on matters of general interest, their activities outside the theatre chronicled; in apparent reaction, some had made a point of their own reclusiveness, their personal inaccessibility. Shaffer took neither colourful path: he kept himself to himself, not particularly secretive but evidently taking the reasonable attitude that his plays were the thing, and any information about his intellectual history and private life that he might care to vouchsafe was strictly coincidental to judgement of the work, and anyway not particularly interesting in itself.

So we know something about his early life, but not very much. He is one of twin brothers (and his twin, Anthony Shaffer, has also become a successful playwright with his ingenious thriller *Sleuth*, but a playwright, evidently, of a very different kind), born in Liverpool. He took a degree at Cambridge and worked for a while in a New York library, then in a London music publishers (in 1961–62 he worked as a music critic for *Time and Tide*, and music was, and evidently from the plays still is, a major interest of Shaffer's). He began writing at Cambridge, or shortly after; accounts differ as to whether he was writing and tearing up plays at that point, or writing and tearing up detective novels. Whichever it was, only three detective novels written with his brother (two of them under a pseudonym) seem to have seen the light of day until 1957, when he managed to get a play he had written for the stage produced on television. In the line, somewhat, of his detective stories, it was a thriller about spies and counterspies battling over an intercontinental ballistic missile, called *Balance of Terror*. It was capable, but not in any way remarkable. A little odder was his second produced play, also for television, *The Salt Lands* (1957), an apparently realistic drama of life in modern Israel which covertly adapts the situations and structure of Greek tragedy to an epic tale of two immigrant brothers, one a prophet-visionary, the other an urban-minded opportunist, who come into murderous conflict on a kibbutz; though the superimposition was rather patchily worked out, the play did have passages of serious and even impassioned writing which stay in the memory.

After which came, seemingly out of the blue, *Five Finger Exercise* (1958). It is a family drama of some intensity, and the obvious (if ultimately unilluminating) question is, is it autobiographical? This is the first question Shaffer was asked in the *Transatlantic Review* interview of 1963. His answer is, as one might expect, yes and no:

All art is autobiographical inasmuch as it refers to personal experience. This is so in both the plays and in the Inca play I have been working on [*The Royal Hunt of the Sun*] . . . The torment of adolescence is in all the plays, as is the essential pessimism in the face of certain death. These tensions and obsessions are auto-biographical. But of course they are dressed up as stories, myths. That is theatre.

And it is as theatre that *Five Finger Exercise* calls for judgement. A rather old-fashioned sort of theatre in many ways: a drawing-room drama set among the *haute bourgeoisie* in a weekend cottage in Suffolk. But as Shaffer reasonably remarked in the same interview:

There are many tunes yet to be written in C major. And there are many plays yet to be written in a living room. As far as the form being old-fashioned, I suppose it is. But *Look Back in Anger* is just as old-fashioned in form. Anyway, form is dictated by content.

(Oddly enough, John Osborne himself described *Look Back in Anger* five years after writing it as 'a formal, rather old-fashioned play'.)

Certainly, directly autobiographical or not, *Five Finger Exercise* is the play of Shaffer's which, up until *Equus* at least, most clearly centres on 'the torment of adolescence'. Though interest (and sympathy) is distributed very evenly among the five characters, there seems to be little doubt that Clive, the nineteen-year-old son of the house, is the central character. He and his younger sister Pamela are the children of impossible parents. Not, perhaps, impossible individually, but together they have turned their children into the battleground on which are fought out the resentments and dissatisfactions of their ill-advised marriage. One can see very easily how they came to be married in the first place: Shaffer shows great skill in creating the whole fabric of a life before our eyes without a lot of heavy exposition and explanation. Evidently at one point sexual attraction was reinforced by a balance of differing attributes which probably seemed to complement each other: Stanley was a handsome, hearty, aggressive, ambitious, very masculine man; Louise was daintily nurtured (if not quite in such grand style as she would now like people to suppose), sensitive, cultured, artistic, very feminine. Now, some twenty years after, she regards him as a blundering oaf, he regards her as an affected bitch.

And the children have to live with this situation as best they may. In particular, they have to try to live their own lives, develop their own personalities, in spite of the constant interference of their parents and the way they are always likely to be used as weapons. Inevitably, there is some reversal of roles: Pamela is a tomboy, more like the sort of son her father might have wished for, while Clive is the sensitive, vulnerable, and, his father would say, effeminate, mother's boy. Both children painfully want the approval (which they take to equal love) of both their parents, and neither, obviously, is going to get it. This seems to disturb Clive a lot more than Pamela, and in his disturbance he becomes his own worst enemy—the more frantically he tries to communicate with his father, the more worried and frightened his father is by his emotionalism, and the less he is likely to approve or understand. Pamela is safer by taking refuge in a certain (possibly calculated) stolidity: she just goes her own way and as far as possible lets the tides of emotion wash over her. Of course, she is only fourteen, and no doubt her time of trial is yet to come.

Into this already explosive situation comes a catalyst, in the shape of Walter Langer, a mature-seeming German of twenty-two, who has been hired by Louise to tutor Pamela in French. He feels like one of the family (which he romanticizes furiously as an ideal happy, balanced English family); he is thoroughly encouraged to feel that way, most effusively and explicitly by Louise, but to some extent by everybody. In this feeling he is cruelly deceived—like the central character in Angus Wilson's terrible play *The Stranger*, he is

6

fated to discover that there can be an unbridgeable gap between being one of the family and being 'just like' one of the family.

Naturally Walter, even if he has stepped into the lion's den, has not come from nowhere. He has, as we gradually discover, his own problems, his own neurotic reasons for his excessive, instant attachment to the Harrington family. It is not, actually, so difficult to guess what these reasons may be, given his absolute refusal to teach German, which seems to be the logical thing for him to do, and his evasive insistence that his parents are dead, his own family background non-existent. Of course his parents are not dead, and of course his reasons for this wholesale rejection of his Germanness have something to do with what he is hiding—that his father was a Nazi who used to beat into him Nazi precepts of anti-Semitism, anti-liberalism, anti-Catholicism with his mother's approval. So much he eventually admits to Clive, partly in self-explanation, partly in order to make him see that his family situation is really not so bad after all.

In his own terms he is probably right—but then, other people's family problems always seem far easier to deal with than one's own. And Walter hardly yet realizes that his prime function in the Harrington family is that of a new toy, and that when they play, they play rough. The first round of the game occurs before we even meet Walter and Pam: it is Stanley baiting Clive because of his arty-tarty friends and airy-fairy ways, and Louise in retaliation baiting him about his coarseness and lack of culture. Round one to the gentle people: Stanley slams out of the house with his golf clubs. After time out for introductions, battle is joined again, again between Stanley and Clive, with Louise intervening and Walter as a partial spectator. This time it is Clive who slams out, leaving Louise to play a rather different game with Walter, a sort of mock-seduction. Clive's return breaks this game up, and next it is Clive attempting another sort of seduction, by tempting Walter to come away with him, to be his special friend. Walter backs, none too gracefully, out of this particular situation, and in consequence Clive brings down the First Act curtain in rousing style by telling Stanley in a fit of jealousy, malice and revenge, that he caught Walter making love to Louise. Game and set, though not yet match, to Clive.

Act Two shows a series of regroupings. Pam talks to Walter about marriage in general and (obviously) her parents' marriage in particular; she is giving him a warning which he does not heed. Clive talks to Walter, with a more direct warning, and in the process elicits the truth about his family situation. Pam also takes it on herself to act as an interpreter of Clive to their father, but without much success. And at this time Walter makes his biggest mistake: pushed by Louise into an avowal of his feelings for her, he blurts out that he regards her as the mother he has never really had. This, of course, is not at all what Louise wants. It is hard to say exactly what she does want: probably not an affair, but at least an impetuous declaration of passion, about which she can feel flattered and act wisely, older-womanly.

The end of this particular round of games is in sight, and it is clear who is going to be the victim. Walter is still blissfully unaware, however, still trying to do his bit by sorting out the problems that the Harringtons, deep down, do not really want sorting out. He offends Pam by treating her too much like a child, he offends Stanley by trying to explain his son to him, and is then totally shattered when Louise gets Stanley to dismiss him, on the flimsy excuse that he is having a bad effect on Pam, and Stanley (on the equally flimsy excuse, which he really does not believe himself, that Walter is having an affair with Louise) carries it a stage further by threatening to have him deported back to Germany. Who is to blame? Everyone, to some extent. And who has anything to gain? Everyone, if they can see the situation rightly. But no one does: the confrontation between Stanley and Louise that might save their marriage ends in an armed truce at best, and the possibility that Clive might be able to get away and stand on his own feet is grimly scotched by Louise, who tries to destroy him by suggesting to him that his denunciation of her and Walter came not from jealousy over her attentions, but from homosexual attraction to Walter. So the most anyone has learnt from the whole interlude is Clive's dawning awareness that he too has claws, he too can hurt and destroy if he wants to.

So far, so good. What Shaffer has given us is, in outline, a thoroughly effective, theatrical, traditional, well-made play. *Five Finger Exercise* is plotted with all the aplomb of a Pinero, getting characters on and off stage with neatly disguised skill and efficiency, planting enough background information without ever bogging us down in wads of obvious exposition, and bringing the curtain down on each of its four scenes with a resounding curtain line. Though it emerged in 1958, it is technically very much part of the mainstream tradition of British drama; it would have been written in much the same way if *Look Back in Anger* and its successors had never happened. And, indeed, it is not necessarily any the worse for that. Its subject matter, if not highly fashionable at the time, was certainly perfectly legitimate, then or at any other time, and the form, as Shaffer remarked, is governed by the content (as well as, to an extent, vice versa).

If one could complain about it (or express doubt at all) it would be on two counts. The first is perhaps largely temporary: the language of the younger characters is full of period slang which has got far enough back to sound dated without as yet taking on a period charm, and, worse, it is the superficial expression of a relationship which has too much heavy whimsy for comfort (we recognize that the playful exchanges between Louise and 'Jou-Jou'/Clive are meant to be embarrassing, but it is hard to be so sure about those between Pamela and Clive). The other cause for complaint may also be rather subjective: it is that, in a period of unmistakably individual, personal drama, Shaffer seems to be resolutely impersonal. By using, as he does, the language of the tribe he may be taking refuge, avoiding the sort of personal commitment (however sublimated in art) from which great drama comes. But then *Five Finger Exercise* is a good, commercial, West End play; at this stage Shaffer is still perfecting his craft, and does not aim or claim to be doing anything more.

Within this definition, though, there is one noticeable oddity the play has, from which, if we observed it, we might wonder whether Shaffer was more than he first appeared to be. That is the way that the play, while functioning (very well) within a tradition which sedulously avoided eloquence, which cultivated the understated, the matter-of-fact (or to put it in more acceptable terms, tended to depend rather heavily on Harold Pinter's second silence, when what is really happening between people is apparently unrelated, or very slightly related, to what they are actually saying), does suddenly burst out every so often into sizzling monologues in which the characters reveal themselves in quite a different way. And not, of course, necessarily any the less natural a way—in 'real life' people often talk in monologue, whenever they are given half a chance (maybe because the other person is not listening anyway)—but certainly by the conventions of 1958 a far less naturalistic way.

The only character who is not given at least one such monologue is Pamela—significantly, her longest speech is to her father about her brother, specifically relating a dream of his, in which he dreams that Stanley is literally (and therefore no doubt metaphorically) stripping him naked. But all the rest get the stage to themselves sooner or later for detailed self-revelation. Near the beginning Louise bares all her rather silly, rather pathetic pretensions to Walter in a long description—romanticized, we later discover—of her Anglo-French family background and upbringing. In response Walter blurts out something of his (also rather romanticized, we may think) regard for England and the English. Next Clive reveals something of his own mocking, would-be disaffected personality in a further long speech setting the record straight on his mother for Walter's benefit, and shortly thereafter makes his most desperate attempt to explain himself to his father, who of course understands nothing of what he is saying. In the second act Walter gets his chances, first to Clive about his true family background, and then, again to Clive, trying to help him by describing his own first sexual encounter. And between these two speeches Stanley gets his say in a furious diatribe about the deceptions and disappointments of having a family, addressed nominally to Walter but really, as the stage direction notes, talking more or less to himself.

All of these big speeches have one thing in common: they tell us something about the great preoccupation of drama during the decade of theatre of the Absurd and all that: communication, its possibilities and impossibilities. Sometimes the speakers want to communicate and fail, sometimes, as with Louise's monologue, what is said is a smokescreen. Rarely do two characters succeed in communicating (perhaps only Clive and Walter manage to get through at all to each other), but if this is so, it is not so much because, as it was fashionable to say at the time, communication is impossible, but (again as Harold Pinter has pointed out) because people who can and do communicate perfectly will often fear to communicate. Stanley could understand what Clive is saying to him—he is not essentially a stupid man—but he does not want to, he fears the challenge it may pose to everything he has built his life on. So he takes refuge in deliberate obtuseness. Walter does not want his illusions about his ideal English family shattered. Clive comes to the point of wanting to hurt other people before they can hurt him too much. The variety of patterns within a single play is astonishing, and already shows a special quality in Shaffer's drama which is not at first glance apparent.

But still, the playwright does not seem to be personally involved in his play to any significant degree. Though his comment about the torment of adolescence might lead us to suppose that he identifies most closely with Clive in the play (which may indeed be the case), he does not slant the play at all in his direction. Depending on our mood or our preconceptions, we could find any of the characters the most sympathetic, the most put-upon (except perhaps the tiresome Louise, but even she emerges ultimately as the victim of her own fantasies). One can certainly understand and sympathize with Stanley's mystification at his own children, Clive's need for the reassurance that his father loves him as well as requiring to be loved, Pam's desire to be treated like the adult she nearly is and not be constantly put down by her mother, Walter's hope that he will be totally accepted by these funny English, that he will understand one day what makes them tick. This balance of sympathy in a dramatist is of course admirable, and makes for effective drama. But might one not be forgiven for wondering if a vital spark of passion was not missing?

If so, Shaffer's next appearance before the theatre-going public did not answer the question one way or the other; rather, it delayed our giving it serious thought and coming to even a provisional conclusion. For although during the following years Shaffer was working away darkly on a major project of his own, what meanwhile emerged was a double bill of almost defiantly lightweight one-act comedies, *The Public Eye* and *The Private Ear*, first produced in London in 1962. Obviously, a couple of distinct snobberies may be operative in our judgement of these plays: those according to which we automatically feel some kind of respect for sheer size in the theatre ('Oh, it's only a one-act play'), and by which we tend to downgrade comedy by comparison with 'serious' drama. Now as it happens, one of Shaffer's masterpieces, *Black Comedy*, is in fact a one-act comedy (if not, even less reputably, a farce). And in the context of this we should perhaps be ready to look rather more closely at these two plays than we otherwise might.

The general feeling seems to be that, of the two, *The Public Eye* is the more successful. Shaffer himself apparently regards *The Private Ear* as a piece that never worked out quite right: it was written in four days, originally as a television play, and rewritten for the American production, and he has never been happy with it. Also, it ran into some criticism of a different sort from people who felt that Shaffer was not quite at home with a cast of working-class characters (it is the only real attempt he has made to deal with one), and that maybe he tended to patronize them slightly. There is, I think, some truth in the first part of the proposition, but none at all in the second. Indeed, though Shaffer seems not quite in his element in details of dialogue expression, there are ways in which the play gives the impression of being one of his most deeply felt, and makes one wonder if it is not rather the direct depiction of humiliation and the defeat of a kind of idealism for which he feels considerable sympathy which ultimately makes him uncomfortable.

Be that as it may, he certainly seems to identify more openly with the awkward, idealistic, unworldly Bob, than with any of his other heroes. Bob's great passion in life is music, classical music. That, and keeping his gramophone (known affectionately as Behemoth) fed with records is the only thing that makes his menial office job acceptable. In music he is secure, controlled and in control; elsewhere he is liable to look like a bumbling idiot. And never more so than when in the company of his very different friend Ted. Ted is the assured, realistic one who knows all the angles, has a way with girls, accepts his life and himself for what they are with no regrets. As he puts it at one point, Bob is:

a good boy. He wouldn't hurt a fly—and that's not because he's a fly himself either. Because he isn't. He's got feelings inside him I wouldn't know anything about . . . Real deep feelings. They're no use to him, of course. They're in his way. If you ask me, you're better off without all that dreamy bit.

The business of the evening on which the action of the play takes place is that Ted shall help Bob counteract that dreamy bit and aid him to make a good impression on a girl he has met at a concert and has decided is his destined soul-mate. Everything is right, from her Botticelli neck to her interest in music. The only problem is, can she be persuaded to take a serious interest in him, over an intimate *dîner à deux* he is staging in his flat, with Ted's assistance? The answer to that question is apparent almost as soon as Doreen arrives. She went to the concert, we soon gather, only because there was a free ticket and it offended her frugal nature to waste it, she knows nothing about music, is painfully out of her depth, and rather frightened by Bob, whom she finds incomprehensible and unaccountable. Ted is much more her type anyway; they can communicate, they both like dancing, they have the same idea of fun. We can see this, Ted can see this, but of course poor Bob, lost in his dreams, cannot.

The inevitable happens. Even with Ted playing reasonably fair, or as fair as can be expected, Bob's gaucherie and failure to grasp the realities of the situation are bound to get him nowhere and he will certainly be left alone at the end, a sadder if, we may suspect, scarcely a wiser man. And so it happens. But along the way the play includes two of Shaffer's most striking scenes. One of them, which contains the germ of his brilliant talent for manipulating the physical

13

possibilities of the theatre (most apparent in *Black Comedy* and *Equus*), is the scene in which not a word is said for some six minutes while Bob and Doreen circle each other warily, come nearly to a meaningful contact and then sharply separate again, all while the music of the love duet from *Madam Butterfly* plays on the gramophone. The other, which almost immediately precedes it, is at the other extreme of highly verbal expression, one of Shaffer's most sustained and deeply felt monologues, in which Bob tries to convey to Doreen something of his feeling (which is no doubt not so different from Shaffer's own feeling) for and about life and music.

BOB. When dad died I came south. If I could start again, I'd *make* myself study.

DOREEN. Well, you could if you wanted. You're still young. You could go to night-school.

BOB. No.

DOREEN. Why not? Your friend does.

BOB. Well, of course, he's got drive. You lot go on about drive, but you can't have drive without enjoying your work. Now Ted does. When he leaves the office he's as fresh as a daisy, but when I come home I've hardly got the energy to grill a chop, let alone pick up a French book; and what have I done? Filled in about sixty invoices. What a way to spend your day, with all the possibilities in you. And some of those people have been doing it for thirty years. Taking endless dictation. Typing thousands of meaningless letters. 10th of the inst. 11th ultimo. C.I.F. E. & O.E. Thanking you in anticipation. Your esteemed order. Are you going to spend the rest of your life typing nonsense, top copy and two carbons?

DOREEN. Well, like I say, we haven't got much choice, have we?

BOB. Yes, we have. We must have. We weren't born to do this. Eyes. Complicated things like eyes, weren't made by God just to see columns of twopence halfpennies written up in a ledger. Tongues. Languages. Good grief, the woman next to me in the office even sounds like a typewriter. A thin, chipped old typewriter, always clattering on about what Miss Story said in accounts and what Burnham said back. It's so wrong! Do you know how many thousands of years it took to make anything so beautiful, so feeling, as your hand? People say 'I know something like the back of my hand', but they don't know their hands.

They wouldn't recognize a photograph of them. Why? Because their hands are anonymous. They're just tools for filling invoices, turning lathes round. They cramp up from picking slag out of moving belts of coal. If that's not blasphemy, what is? . . . I'll tell you something really daft. Some nights when I come back here I give Behemoth a record for his supper. That's the way I look at him sometimes, feeding off discs, you know. And I conduct it. If it's a concerto I play the solo part, running up and down the keyboard, doing the expressive bits, everything. I imagine someone I love is sitting out in the audience watching; you know, someone I want to admire me. . . Anyway, it sort of frees things inside me. At great moments I feel shivery all over. It's marvellous to feel shivery like that. What I want to know is, why can't I feel that in my work? Why can't I—oh, I don't know—feel bigger? There's something in me I know that's big. That can be excited, anyway. And that must mean I can excite other people, if only I knew what way . . . I never met anyone to show me that way.

Compared with this outburst *The Public Eye*, though much more poised and obviously accomplished, is certainly much lighter. But by no means negligible. It is also a three-character piece, about a stuffy husband who has (somewhat against his better judgement) hired a private detective to spy on his wife and find out if there is, as he suspects, another man. By this time there is, even though the relationship is unbelievably innocent and remote: the 'other man' is the detective, whose presence has been observed by the wife (though not understood) and developed into a distant, non-speaking companionship between them as they wander the streets of London together, if still apart. The showpiece of the play is the eccentric character of the detective, an elfin Greek with an uncontrollable sweet tooth which keeps him constantly nibbling out of paper bags—particularly when nervous.

What the play is really about is a breakdown of communication in a marriage. Belinda is upset by Charles's

. . . iceberg voice. I can't bear it. 'One would hardly say' 'I scarcely think' 'One might hazard, my dear'. All that morning-suit language. It's only hiding.

Why has the man she loved and married turned into a stuffed shirt? What happened to all the fun and surprise? Why does she have to feel, as Clive does in relation to his father in *Five Finger Exercise*, watched, guilty, responsible, *examined*? Naturally, Charles suggests it is not all his fault:

Let me tell you something. Each man has all those things inside him, sex, jokes, jazz and many more important things than that. He's got the whole of human history in him, only in capsule. But it takes someone who loves him to make those capsules grow. If they don't grow, he's not loved enough. And that kind of love can only be given by an adult.

The solution to their problem, engineered by Cristoforou, a whimsical and capricious *deus ex machina*, is that he and Charles have to change places (rather like the husband and the outsider in Pinter's *A Slight Ache*, only here the exchange is explained and rationalized). Charles and Belinda must wander wordlessly round the streets of London, showing each other things and taking each other places, for a whole month. Charles kicks against it, but he accepts: by playing an unlikely role, perhaps he will make some unlikely capsules grow. Otherwise, like the Yaghan Indians Belinda speaks of earlier on, all he can expect to do is be scrapped by nature, fail like the crops, and sit on green water, waiting to die.

Indians were evidently already in Shaffer's mind, with reason, since he had been working for some time on various drafts of the play which finally reached the stage in 1964 as *The Royal Hunt of the Sun*. Originally it was intended for the Royal Shakespeare Company, but they seem to have been daunted by the magnitude of the production and size of the cast, and after some further rewriting (each draft, it seems, gained in clarity and simplicity compared with its predecessor) it was taken on by the National Theatre, to become one of their most remarkable popular successes. It is at once a spectacular drama and a think-piece written in rather elaborate literary terms. As Shaffer himself summarized its theme in an interview[1] shortly before it was produced, it is 'a play about two men: one of them is an atheist, and the

[1] *Plays and Players*, April 1964.

other is a god'. The atheist is Pizarro, Spanish conqueror of Peru, and the god is the Inca Atahuallpa.

Again to quote Shaffer,

The play is about the relationship, intense, involved and obscure, between these two men, one of whom is the other's prisoner: they are so different, and yet in many ways—they are both bastards, both usurpers, both unscrupulous men of action, both illiterate—they are mirror images of each other. And the theme which lies behind their relationship is the search for God—the search for a definition of the idea of God. In fact, the play is an attempt to define the concept of God.

In other terms, Shaffer has explained that the vital thought process behind the play was that he:

felt more and more inclined to draw the character Pizarro, who is a Catholic, as an atheist, or at least as a man who explores what and who he is. When the Church is revealed to him as being wicked and suspect, and loyalty, friendship, is revealed as being suspect and wicked, he has a feeling of the meaninglessness of life. It is this: what can one ultimately find to give one strength and stability?[1]

All of which makes the play sound rather heavy going, and certainly unlikely material to have the makings of a major London and Broadway success. That it nevertheless turned out to be just that probably has quite a lot to do with the spectacular element, itself welcome in a theatre starved— the musical apart—of spectacle. But even more important, of course, is the way the spectacle was handled in John Dexter's brilliant production and Michael Annals's extraordinary setting, with its transformable sun-motif which could close into a great medallion with the emblem of the *conquistadores* incised on it. This was a central feature as telling as the revolving set-piece in *Oliver*,[2] and contributed greatly to the realization on stage of Shaffer's original intention, 'a kind of "total" theatre, involving not only words but rites, mimes, masks and magics'. It is, he modestly

[1] *Behind the Scenes: Theatre and Film Interviews from the 'Transatlantic Review'*, ed. J. F. McCrindle, 1971.

[2] A highly successful musical of the 1960s based on Dickens's *Oliver Twist*.

17

observes in his author's notes to the published text, 'a director's piece, a pantomimist's piece, a musician's piece, a designer's piece, and of course an actor's piece, almost as much as it is an author's'.

Clearly Shaffer has progressed a long way in his dramatic thinking from the easy naturalism of *Five Finger Exercise*. *The Royal Hunt of the Sun* is a chronicle play covering a period of over four years and many thousands of miles journeying. It is, for all that, quite tightly organized, but evidently all the material could not be encompassed in a naturalistic drama—it can be done only by calling on all the resources of the theatre, deriving techniques partly from Kabuki, partly from Shakespeare's way with history, partly from Brechtian epic theatre. The central thread of the drama is the mental and spiritual development of Pizarro, culminating in his strange relationship with Atahuallpa, his mirror image, the god he has caught in his net. After these two characters the most important is Martin, Pizarro's retainer, who as old Martin acts as narrator for us and as young Martin undergoes the torments of adolescence, the slow, ugly process of learning by disenchantment, reconciling one's ideals with the harsh realities of life.

Pizarro begins to teach him early, before the expedition has begun, when he has only just recruited his men:

PIZARRO. Listen to them. There's the world. The eagle rips the condor; the condor rips the crow. And the crow would blind all the eagles in the sky if once it had the beak to do it. The clothed hunt the naked; the legitimates hunt the bastards, and put down the word Gentleman to blot up the blood. Your Chivalry laws don't govern me, Martin. They're for belonging birds—like them legitimate birds with claws trim on the perch their fathers left them. Make no error; if I could once peck them off it, I'd tear them into gobbets to feed cats. Don't ever trust me, boy.

YOUNG MARTIN. Sir? I'm your man.

PIZARRO. Don't ever trust me. . . . Or if you must, never say I deceived you. Know me.

YOUNG MARTIN. I do sir. You are all I ever want to be.

PIZARRO. I am nothing you could ever want to be, or any man alive. Believe this: if the time ever came for you to harry me, I'd rip you too, easy as look at you. Because you belong too, Martin.

YOUNG MARTIN. I belong to you, sir!
PIZARRO. You belong to hope. To faith. To priests and pre-
tences. To dipping flags and ducking heads; to laying hands and
licking rings; to powers and parchments; and the whole vast
stupid congregation of crowners and cross-kissers. You're a
worshipper, Martin. A groveller. You were born with feet but
you prefer your knees. It's you who make Bishops—Kings—
Generals. You trust me, I'll hurt you past believing.

As will be observed, Shaffer's Pizarro is a great talker (the
style of these speeches, with their cunning repetitions and
echoes, is a fair sample of the play's texture), one of the
world's explorers, mental as well as physical. He has tried
everything, thought about everything, been disgusted or
disenchanted by everything. Here he is on death:

Fame is long. Death is longer. . . Does anyone ever die for
anything? I thought so once. Life was fierce with feeling. It was
all hope, like on that boy. Swords shone, and armour sang, and
cheese bit you, and kissing burned and Death—ah, death was
going to make an exception in my case. I couldn't believe I was
ever going to die. But once you know it—really know it—it's all
over. You know you've been cheated, and nothing's the same
again.

And here on time:

Listen, listen! Everything we feel is made of Time. All the
beauties of life are shaped by it. Imagine a fixed sunset: the last
note of a song that hung an hour, or a kiss for half of it. Try and
halt a moment in our lives and it becomes maggoty at once. Even
that word 'moment' is wrong, since that would mean a speck of
time, something you could pick up on a rag and peer at . . . But
that's the awful trap of life. You can't escape maggots unless you
go with Time. And if you go, they wriggle in you anyway.

And yet, like Tennyson's Ulysses, he has never ceased
from searching. For what? Most of all, perhaps, for some-
ting to believe in, something by which he can cheat time
and overcome the only ultimate reality, death. It is a curious
fate which brings him, nominally in search of gold, fame and
a place in history, across hundreds of miles of privation, to
the land of the Inca Atahuallpa, of which he can claim
'Not a leaf stirs in my kingdom without my leave'. For

19

Atahuallpa might be the something he can believe in—'He has some meaning for me, this man-God'. And, paradoxically, Pizarro might be something for Atahuallpa to believe in, the white god from the east who will inaugurate a new era. The core of the drama takes place in the tranced stillness when Pizarro has Atahuallpa a prisoner ('What do worshippers do when you snatch their god? They do nothing') and Atahuallpa has Pizarro enthralled by his own conviction that he cannot die, that he rules death and, at the reappearance of his father the sun, he too will rise again.

It is in this situation that Pizarro the man of action finds himself for once ineffectual and indecisive. He admires the Inca civilization, to a point that one of the accompanying priests, De Nizza, finds blasphemous.

DE NIZZA. . . . Look hard, you *will* find Satan here, because here is a country which denies the right to hunger.
PIZARRO. You call hunger a right?
DE NIZZA. Of course, it gives life meaning. Look around you: happiness has no feel for men here since they are forbidden unhappiness. They have everything in common, so they have nothing to give each other. They are part of the seasons, no more; as indistinguishable as mules, as predictable as trees. All men are born unequal: this is a divine gift. And want is their birthright. Where you deny this and there is no hope of any new love; where tomorrow is abolished, and no man ever thinks 'I can change myself', there you have the rule of Anti-Christ.

But Pizarro is not convinced:

DE NIZZA. When I came here first I thought I had found Paradise. Now I know it is Hell. A country which castrates its people. What are your Inca's subjects? A population of eunuchs, living entirely without choice.
PIZARRO. And what are your Christians? Unhappy hating men. Look: I'm a peasant, I want value for money. If I go marketing for Gods, who do I buy? The God of Europe with all its death and blooding, or Atahuallpa of Peru? His spirit keeps an Empire sweet and still as corn in the field.
DE NIZZA. And you're content to be a stalk of corn?
PIZARRO. Yes, yes! They're no fools, these sun men. They know what cheats you sell on your barrow. Choice. Hunger. Tomorrow. They've looked at your wares and passed on. They live here as part of nature, no hope and no despair.

DE NIZZA. And no life. Why must you be so dishonest? You are not only part of nature and you know it. There is something in you at war with nature; there is in all of us. Something that does not belong in you the animal. What do you think it is? What is this pain in you that month after month makes you hurl yourself against the cage of time? This is God, driving you to accept divine eternity. Take it, General: not this pathetic copy of eternity the Incas have tried to make on earth. Peru is a sepulchre of the soul. For the sake of the free spirit in each of us it must be destroyed.

At the last, inevitably, Pizarro is cheated. The Inca does not rise again, his empire falls in ruins, and soon afterwards Pizarro, who himself unwillingly and incredulously brought this all about, falls too. The play makes its points eloquently, to the extent of being overtalkative were Shaffer's words not complemented by something more, something in the physical staging which balances and enriches the verbal debate. Anyone who saw the original productions will remember the way they looked, the extraordinary impression they created of a meeting of two worlds in a dead, empty space brought to life by the magic of the theatre, long after any argument about the philosophical profundity of the words (or their culpable lack of it) has been forgotten.

The Royal Hunt of the Sun was a *tour de force*, to be followed a year later on the same open stage at Chichester by the same National Theatre Company with another, in its own way perhaps even more extraordinary, *Black Comedy*. This is a piece of physical theatre at its most exhilaratingly virtuoso, based on an idea of dazzling simplicity. From seeing a Chinese theatre company in action, Shaffer had retained the image of actors creating the idea of darkness by miming it. And from this grew the idea of making a farce by simply reversing the normal light values. The play begins in, for the audience, complete darkness, but evidently by what we hear from the stage the characters of the play are happily able to see. After a few moments' conversation, though, all the lights go out for the characters, and all come on for us. From there on we, the audience, are able to watch what nobody within the play can see, until at the end light is restored to them and taken away from us in the final blackout.

What happens in this pool of light between the two darknesses is all very much in the familiar farcical tradition. Brindsley Miller, an impecunious artist, is out to impress the very correct military father of his new debby fiancée, whom he is about to meet for the first time. For this purpose he has decked out his studio flat with antique furniture 'borrowed' from an absent antique-dealer neighbour. Also, an eccentric millionaire collector is coming to see Brindsley's sculptures, this same evening. At which point the lights fuse. The girl's father does arrive, and so eventually does the millionaire, but not before a philosophically inclined electrical repair man has been embarrassingly mistaken for him. There are also some unscheduled visitors, including the prim spinster from upstairs (with a secret taste for gin, more than adequately indulged during the blackout) and, much worse, Harold Gorringe, Brindsley's ladylike neighbour and owner of the furniture, which has therefore to be covertly removed, piece by piece, before the lights can go on again, and Clea, Brindsley's recently discarded girl friend, on mischief bent. The action requires split-second timing and steely nerves on the part of the actors not to flinch noticeably just before they fall down stairs or make painful contact with some to them invisible obstacle. As a piece of sheer theatrical machinery the play is impeccable, as brilliant as anything Shaffer has ever done. And almost indestructible: even in a far less than perfect production the structure carries the play.

It would be labouring a point about this sublimely easy-seeming piece to try to maintain that there is 'something more' to it. But Shaffer is not the sort of writer who can leave his evident intelligence in the cloakroom along with his coat and hat. Inevitably there are points of connexion with his other plays, ideas that carry over. The colonel in *Black Comedy* suggests a more comic re-examination of Stanley in *Five Finger Exercise*. And Bob's remarks in *The Private Ear* about the beauty of hands and people's inability to recognize even their own because they have never really looked at them are reflected vividly in the 'kinky game' Clea devises of guess-the-hand in *Black Comedy*, which gives rise incidentally to a moment of strange resonance when Harold, of all people, proves instantly able to recognize Brindsley's hand in the dark (is it possible that this figure of fun is, under it all, the only character able to step far enough out of his farcical context to have some real intense feeling about someone else?). Miss Furnival from upstairs is also given at one point a drunken monologue of splendid irrelevance to all that is going on around her, which in Shaffer's best manner captures and holds like a bee in amber her character and her class-situation in the smallest possible space:

Prams! Prams! Prams! in the supermarket. All those hideous wire prams, full of babies and bottles! Cornflakes over there is all they say, and then they leave you to yourself! Biscuits over there! (*Pointing in different directions, like a mad signpost*) Cat food over there. Fishcakes over there. Airwick over there! Pink stamps, green stamps, television dinners, pay as you go out—oh, Daddy, it's awful! And then the Godless ones, heathens in their leather jackets, laughing me to scorn! But not for long, oh, no! Who shall stand when He appeareth? He'll strike them from their motor-cycles! He'll dash their helmets to the ground. Yea, wearily, I say unto thee—there shall be an end to gasoline! An end to petroleum! An end to cigarette puffing and jostling with hips. Keep off! Keep off! Keep off! It's shameful! Off! Off! Off!

In the room, Clea's 'magic dark room, where everything happens the wrong way round', a surprising amount of light is after all shed on a surprising collection of characters.

Shaffer's next play generates more heat than light, and not really very much of either. It is published in two versions, *White Lies*, as it was originally produced in New York in a double bill with *Black Comedy*, and *The White Liars*, the final version produced in England in 1968. Neither is very satisfactory: the most striking change between the two is the addition of the tape-recorded voice of the old seaside fortune-teller's long lost Greek lover, which haunts her dreams. All the characters are telling lies, mostly to themselves. The fortune-teller is a middle-European Jew pretending to be a baroness and trying to force a similar fantasy (in tape-recorded flashback) on her lover. The first of her two clients, a pop-star's manager,

tells her a long spiel about how he has suffered from anticipation of his wife's infidelity with his charmingly ruthless
charge, and persuades her to put the fear of God (or something) into the latter. The second client, the pop-star, at
first reacts with all the required superstitious wonderment
at how the baroness can know so much about his deprived
childhood etc., and then, in an ingenious *coup de théâtre*,
turns the tables by bursting into helpless laughter and
telling her the true story of his eminently respectable
middle-class background and his imposture in order to get
notice in a world where only working-class glamour gets
you places. (It is as though Clive from *Five Finger Exercise*
has decided for career purposes to pass himself off as Ted
from *The Private Ear*.) The speech in which Tom, the
pop-star, lays his cards on the table, is a great set-piece for an
actor, but otherwise *The White Liars* is the feeblest piece by
Shaffer to remain in circulation.

Though not, even so, a commercial failure. This fate—
the first time it happened to Shaffer—was reserved for his
next full-length play, *The Battle of Shrivings*. The text of
this as originally performed has not been published, and
Shaffer has subsequently reworked the play for his own
satisfaction and a possible American production under the
title of *Shrivings;* this as yet unperformed version has been
published. The original was admittedly unsatisfactory. The
idea is again, as in *The Royal Hunt of the Sun*, a head-on confrontation between two different ways of life, two opposing
approaches to the business of living. But on this occasion the
matter is talked out rather than acted out, and consequently
the play seems to be lacking a dimension. It is not necessary
to consider *The Royal Hunt of the Sun* or *Equus*, the two
full-length plays which flank *The Battle of Shrivings* in
Shaffer's work, with too much emphasis on the value or
profundity of their philosophical ideas as ideas, because
what is most fascinating about them is their brilliant
visualization of these ideas in terms of theatrical event.
But *The Battle of Shrivings* is a talk- and think-piece very
much as many of Shaw's later plays are; it forces us to
consider the ideas as ideas, and as such they tend to seem
shallow and superficial.

The two characters whose views of life conflict in the play are Sir Gideon, a sort of Bertrand Russell character who has lived out his life as a philosopher and pacifist, and is now universally revered as something of secular saint, and Mark, an ex-pupil of his, now a showily bohemian, almost equally famous poet (as it might be, Robert Graves or Laurence Durrell) who after a long period out of England, writing on Corfu, has come back to be received into the arms of the Establishment with a prize from Oxford University and also, possibly, into the arms of Mother Church. The prim, chaste, humanistic philosophy of Sir Gideon is anathema to him, and he declares war upon it over a weekend spent in Sir Gideon's pacifist, vegetarian home; if Sir Gideon can keep his cool during that time, and consistently turn the other cheek, then Mark will reconvert to humanism.

The 'battle', therefore, is a baiting game. Mark savagely insults Sir Gideon's wife during a 'death game' derived from R. D. Laing (an influence to assume even greater importance in *Equus*), seduces the girl friend of his son, and publicly announces that the son is illegitimate. Gideon takes it all, and so seems to win the battle, but in the process loses a lot of his own faith, even to the extent of striking his own wife, so that by the end the antagonists have changed places. So far, so reasonably good. Unfortunately the play was far too heavily talky, and none of the characters really came to life (except maybe the son, whose cool manner of dealing with his relations and relationships suggests a Clive from *Five Finger Exercise* who has surmounted the torments of adolescence and managed actually to grow up). Mark was little more than his cloak and his swagger; Gideon, prim, whimsical and rather chilly, seemed to have strayed out of one of C. P. Snow's Civil Service novels, and though we were often told that he is a world-famous philosopher he never said anything (let alone did anything) to convince us that this might possibly be so.

In his rewriting of the play for the published text Shaffer has certainly made it more consistent, and intensified its overall gesture. Starting from the structure, he has decided that the character of Gideon's wife was insufficiently developed and perhaps essentially irrelevant, and so eliminated her: Gideon now becomes a divorcee, and the motives for his wife's leaving him are left in the air, one more topic on which Mark can torment him and the rest of the household. (Was it because Gideon's determination on chastity was too much for her? Was it because Gideon was really interested only in young Mediterranean boys?). The removal of the wife means that Gideon has to strike someone else at the end, that someone else has to be savagely humiliated in the death game with the apples. And the obvious object is the eager young American girl disciple, who now takes on much more prominence and much more life in the play.

Recognizing perhaps that one of the play's major flaws was its uncertain hovering between naturalism and a more extravagant rhetorical style, Shaffer has chosen in the reworking to key it up rather than play it down. Gideon becomes less of the uninvolved sage, more believably a man who has fought and is still fighting a battle with emotions which he intellectually rejects. Even the already extravagant character of Mark has been keyed up somewhat, so that one senses his torment, from which his destructive urges arise, as more genuine, that he is in fact much less in control of what he says and does to prove his point than seemed to be the case in the first version. His son David remains rather a sympathetic cypher, but even he is less cool than he was, more emotional, to the point that one can believe that Mark's announcement that his mother was a whore and that David is not his son (a lie, of course, as David recognizes even at the time) could have a traumatic effect on him.

The effect of the play, here as elsewhere throughout, has been moved further from statement (David is upset because his father announces that he is a bastard) towards a different dimension of psychological truth (David is upset because of the complex motivation his father would have in inventing such a lie). It is hard to know how the new version would play on stage—it would need a very careful and precise choice of style for its production and playing—but at any rate to read and imagine on the stage of one's own mind it is far more satisfactory. And far more clearly in the line of Shaffer's development towards *Equus*.

In this connexion, a significant aspect of even the first version of *Shrivings* is the appearance in it of ideas derived from the psychologist R. D. Laing. It would seem that in the later 1960s Shaffer has taken increasing interest in psychology as an intellectual discipline with philosophical ramifications. In 1967 he wrote a full-length television play about a middle-aged Professor of English undergoing a psychological crisis while experimenting with LSD in Greenwich Village; he described it as 'a play in which life is seen through the eyes of the old'. It was written in a 'Joycean, stream-of-consciousness style' and, whether because it was considered too obscure, too controversial or merely too expensive, it never reached production. In 1973 appeared another play based on psychological researches, *Equus*, but this time, though verbally it is in places highly developed and breaks out into real eloquence, it is a piece which only fully exists in the theatre, in terms of the astonishing visual imaging of the action and the way the thought is precipitated into meaningful, unparaphrasable happening.

In this respect *Equus* remains, with, in its very different register, *Black Comedy*, Shaffer's most impressive achievement in the theatre. Like *Black Comedy* and *The Royal Hunt of the Sun*, it was first directed by John Dexter at the National Theatre, and though no doubt there are in theory many ways of directing all three plays, for anyone who saw the first production the stage embodiment of Shaffer's text remains ineffaceable. The action of the play was inspired, Shaffer tells us in his note to the published text, by a real-life case of which he was once told the bare outlines—that a highly disturbed young man had inexplicably blinded a number of horses—and no more. This occurrence has been woven into a texture obviously suggested by (or at least heavily influenced by) R. D. Laing's idea that (to oversimplify drastically) conventional modern psychiatry has been unconsciously moulded by the Establishment into a tool for social manipulation, for preserving the 'norm'.

The two principal characters of the play are Dysart, a middle-aged psychiatrist, and Alan Strang, the disturbed youth who has committed the shocking and mysterious crime. The form in which the subject is treated is very free:

evidently this is the complete confirmation of Shaffer's remarks in relation to *Five Finger Exercise* and the first double bill in the *Transatlantic Review* interview:

I'm very grateful for the training I've had with these two plays. I've learned how to tell a story, draw characters, devise plausible entrances and exits. I've acquired a technique to stand me in good stead for the greater and less charted seas of semi- and expressionistic theatre.

The action takes place on a bare, darkened stage with a few basic props which are grouped and regrouped in view of the audience. Dysart acts as a sort of narrator, stepping in and out of the action, which flows freely backwards and forwards in time. And, most important, there are the horses constantly present in sight and sound, invading the psyche of the characters and providing a sort of chorus of sounds: the 'Equus noise' which consists of 'humming, thumping and stamping—though never of neighing or whinnying'. The horses are seen as conventionalized creatures of theatrical ritual: Shaffer's note on their treatment is revealing enough to deserve quotation in its entirety:

The actors wear track-suits of chestnut velvet. On their feet are light strutted hooves, about four inches high, set on metal horse-shoes. On their hands are gloves of the same colour. On their heads are tough masks made of alternating bands of silver wire and leather: their eyes are outlined by leather blinkers. The actors' own heads are seen beneath them: no attempt should be made to conceal them.
Any literalism which could suggest the cosy familiarity of a domestic animal—or worse, a pantomime horse—should be avoided. The actors should never crouch on all fours, or even bend forward. They must always—except on the one occasion where Nugget is ridden—stand upright, as if the body of the horse extended invisibly behind them. Animal effect must be created entirely mimetically, through the use of legs, knees, neck, face and the turn of the head which can move the mask above it through all the gestures of equine wariness and pride. Great care must also be taken that the masks are put on before the audience with very precise timing—the actors watching each other, so that the masking has an exact and ceremonial effect.

And what Shaffer shows us with this machinery—*shows*

us, not really tells us—is the process of Alan Strang's gradual deviation from the respectable norm, into neurosis and a crime of cruelty to animals which is found universally shocking, inexplicable and prima facie evidence for his insanity and desperate need for psychiatric treatment which may be hoped to restore him to 'normality'. Linked with this in the play's loose-seeming yet taut and economical structure is a progressive demonstration of the hollowness and self-questioning of Dysart, the psychiatrist who is charged with this job of mental restoration. Shaffer does not make the elementary mistake, any more than R. D. Laing does, of romanticizing madness into a vision of the truth denied to the 'sane', but he does show us Alan's particular brand of insanity as a legitimate and valuable response to experience which brings its own benefits and has to be emasculated by society in the cause of self-preservation: Dysart, with his arid, uncommunicative relations with his wife, his academic devotion to his pet dream-world of classical Greek antiquity, comes eventually to a recognition that at the very least 'That boy has known a passion more ferocious than I have felt in any second of my life'.

The passion is for the dark god of his own creation, Equus, an amalgam of his first traumatic experience of ecstasy when given a ride on a horse by a passing stranger and his masochistic devotion to the suffering, humiliated image of Christ offered to him by his mother's morbid religiosity. In the battle of his family background between his mother's refined, long-suffering religious beliefs and his father's brusque, self-educated atheism both parties have one thing in common: a repressive puritanism and a related inability to cope with expressions of emotion. His father, as Alan discovers shortly before he commits the crime, takes refuge in blue movies which he affects to regard with horror and disgust: his mother prays to a God made in her own image. Neither can understand their son's development towards his own private mythology of Equus and his servant horses, the god of fierceness and fire and beauty, the jealous god whose temple must not be sullied by human sexual contacts, whose watchers must be blinded lest they see too much.

At one level the blinding lends itself to pat Freudian formulations. Alan's parents have forced him to suppress and so divert his normal sexual drives, so when he finds himself sexually involved with a girl at the stables where he works, his build-up of guilt finds expression in destructive action against the horse-god as embodiment of his own super-ego. The crime thus brings his secret world out into the open, and puts him in direct conflict with society. At which point Dysart has to take action, to enact the sacrifice required of him by society to the great god Normal—'a murderous, non-existent phantom'. And what, exactly is he sacrificing?

DYSART: (quietly) Can you think of anything worse one can do to anybody than take away their worship?
HESTHER: Worship?
DYSART: Yes, that word again!
HESTHER: Aren't you being a little extreme?
DYSART: Extremity's the point.
HESTHER: Worship isn't destructive, Martin. I know that.
DYSART: I don't. I only know it's the core of his life. What else has he got? Think about him. He can hardly read. He knows no physics or engineering to make the world real for him. No paintings to show him how others have enjoyed it. No music except television jingles. No history except tales from a desperate mother. No friends. Not one kid to give him a joke, or make him know himself more moderately. He's a modern citizen for whom society doesn't exist. He lives *one hour* every three weeks—howling in a mist. And after the service kneels to a slave who stands over him obviously and unthrowably his master. With my body I thee worship! . . . Many men have less vital relationships with their wives.

And to what result?

My desire might be to make this boy an ardent husband—a caring citizen—a worshipper of abstract and unifying God. My achievement, however, is more likely to make a ghost! . . . Let me tell you exactly what I'm going to do to him!
He steps out of the square and walks round the upstage end of it, storming at the audience.
I'll heal the rash on his body. I'll erase the welts cut into his mind by flying manes. When that's done, I'll put him on a metal

scooter, and send him puttering off into the modern world, and he'll never touch hide again! I'll give him the modern, Normal world where animals are treated properly—tethered all their lives in dim light, for example, just to feed it. I'll take away his Field of Ha Ha, and give him Normal places for his ecstasy—six-lane motorways driven through the guts of cities, extinguishing Place altogether, *even the idea of Place*! I'll give him the nourishing, earthy, Normal world where land is cemented over from one sea to the next, and sea itself lies dead—all holy waters—Aegean, Ionian, Tyrrhenian waters—stinking dead under three inches of sun tan oil! . . . With any luck, his private parts will come to feel as plastic to him as the products of the factory to which he will almost certainly be sent. Who knows? He may even come to find sex funny. Smirky funny. Bit of grunt funny. Trampled, and furtive, and entirely in control. Hopefully, he'll feel nothing at his fork but Approved Flesh. *I doubt, however, with much passion*! (Pause) Passion, you see, can be destroyed by a doctor. It cannot be created.

He addresses Alan directly in farewell.

You won't gallop any more, Alan. Horses will be quite safe. You'll save your pennies every week, till you can change that scooter in for a car, and put the odd fifty P on the gee-gees, quite forgetting that they were ever anything more to you than bearers of little profits and little losses. You will, however, be without pain. More or less completely without pain.

Is this good enough? Is this enough? What are these truths against the truth of Alan's own strange experience? The questions continue to vibrate after the play is over. But the fact that they do so is not so much because of Shaffer's verbal formulations, eloquent though they be. It is because in the play we ourselves have lived through Alan's experience with him, we have experienced vicariously some of his ecstasy in naked, pulsing contact with his god, we have made our own oblation to the dark gods of his dreams. The theatrical experience the play offers is mind-enlarging because it gets at our minds through our emotions, our instincts. It does not expound Laing's theories, it inexorably shows them worked out in practice, and silences argument. Its theatrical logic and power are unarguable, and if something of our instinctive response seeps into our intellect subliminally, that is probably no bad thing. At any rate,

Antonin Artaud, who in his formulation of a Theatre of Cruelty imaged the drama as so many immolations with actors and audience signalling to each other through the flames, would have had every reason to be proud of Shaffer as, in this play, one of his most eloquent and effective disciples.

It is an extraordinary development, from the sober, old-fashioned, intelligent but scarcely profound formulations of *Five Finger Exercise* to the equally controlled yet in effect explosive expression of *Equus*. And this last play is of the theatre, theatrical: one cannot conceive it working in any other context, any more than one could *Black Comedy*—certainly not, for instance, in the cinema, where *Five Finger Exercise*, *The Royal Hunt of the Sun*, *The Private Ear* (as *The Pad—And How to Use it*) and *The Public Eye* (as *Follow Me*) have all found second, if none too comfortable, homes. At the outset of Shaffer's theatrical career it was possible to admire his work, to qualify that admiration on account of his seeming lack of emotional commitment to what he was writing about, to pigeon-hole him as a safely accomplished technical conservative and leave it at that. But his gradual, unsparing exploration of the expressive possibilities of his chosen form, in which technical experiment has been accompanied by (necessitated by, no doubt, since as Shaffer says, the content dictates the form) an uncompromising rethinking of the material proper for drama, his own as well as anyone else's, has little by little established him as a major figure in world drama, a theatrical thinker who triumphantly escapes all narrow definitions and ends up a unique phenomenon, like nobody but himself. After *Five Finger Exercise* we might have agreed that the play was 'promising', and felt pretty certain that we knew exactly what it promised. After *Equus* there is just no guessing what he may do next, but it seems inevitable that it will be grand and glorious.

PETER SHAFFER

A Select Bibliography

(Place of publication London, unless otherwise stated)

Collected Editions:

THE PRIVATE EAR, AND, THE PUBLIC EYE: Two one act plays (1962).

BLACK COMEDY, INCLUDING WHITE LIES: Two plays; New York (1967)
—*White Lies*, the first version of *The White Liars*, was not elsewhere
published in its original form.

THE WHITE LIARS. BLACK COMEDY: Two plays (1968).

EQUUS. SHRIVINGS: Two plays; New York (1974).

Separate Works:

THE WOMAN IN THE WARDROBE: A Light-hearted detective story, by
Peter Antony [Anthony Shaffer and Peter Shaffer] (1951). *Novel*
—with drawings by Nicholas Bentley.

HOW DOTH THE LITTLE CROCODILE? A Mr Verity detective story, by
Peter Antony [Anthony Shaffer and Peter Shaffer] (1952). *Novel*

WITHERED MURDER, by A. and P. Shaffer (1955). *Novel*

FIVE FINGER EXERCISE: A Play in two acts and four scenes (1958)
—also published in *New English Dramatists, 4*, 1962.

THE PRIVATE EAR: A Play in one act (1962).

THE PUBLIC EYE: A Play in one act (1962).

THE ROYAL HUNT OF THE SUN: A Play concerning the conquest of
Peru (1964).

THE WHITE LIARS: A Play (1967).

BLACK COMEDY: A Comedy (1967).

EQUUS: A Play (1973).

SHRIVINGS: A Play (1974)
—a revised version of the play originally produced as *The Battle of
Shrivings*.

Critical Studies:

NEW TRENDS IN 20TH CENTURY DRAMA: A Survey since Ibsen and
Shaw, by F. Lumley (1967)
—includes a discussion of Shaffer's work.

THE THIRD THEATRE, by R. Brustein (1969)
—includes a critique of *The Royal Hunt of the Sun*.

ANGER AND AFTER: A Guide to the new British drama, by J. Russell Taylor; revised ed. (1969)
—contains a chapter on Shaffer.
'Like a woman they keep going back to', by R. Hayman, *Drama*, Autumn 1970.
THE CONTEMPORARY THEATRE: The Significant playwrights of our time, by A. Lewis; New York, revised ed. (1971).
'The Plays of Peter Shaffer: Experiment in convention', by C. A. Pennel, *Kansas Quarterly*, iii, 1971.
CONTEMPORARY DRAMATISTS, ed. J. Vinson (1973)
—includes an article and a bibliography of Shaffer's works by J. Elsom.

Interviews:
'Shaffer and the Incas', *Plays and Players*, April 1964
—Peter Shaffer interviewed by John Russell Taylor.
BEHIND THE SCENES: Theatre and film interviews from the *Transatlantic Review*, ed. J. F. McCrindle (1971)
—records an interview by Barry Pree in 1963.
'Philip Oakes talks to Peter Shaffer', *Sunday Times*, 29 July 1973.
'High horse', *The Guardian*, 6 August 1973.
—Peter Shaffer interviewed by C. Ford.

34

WRITERS AND THEIR WORK